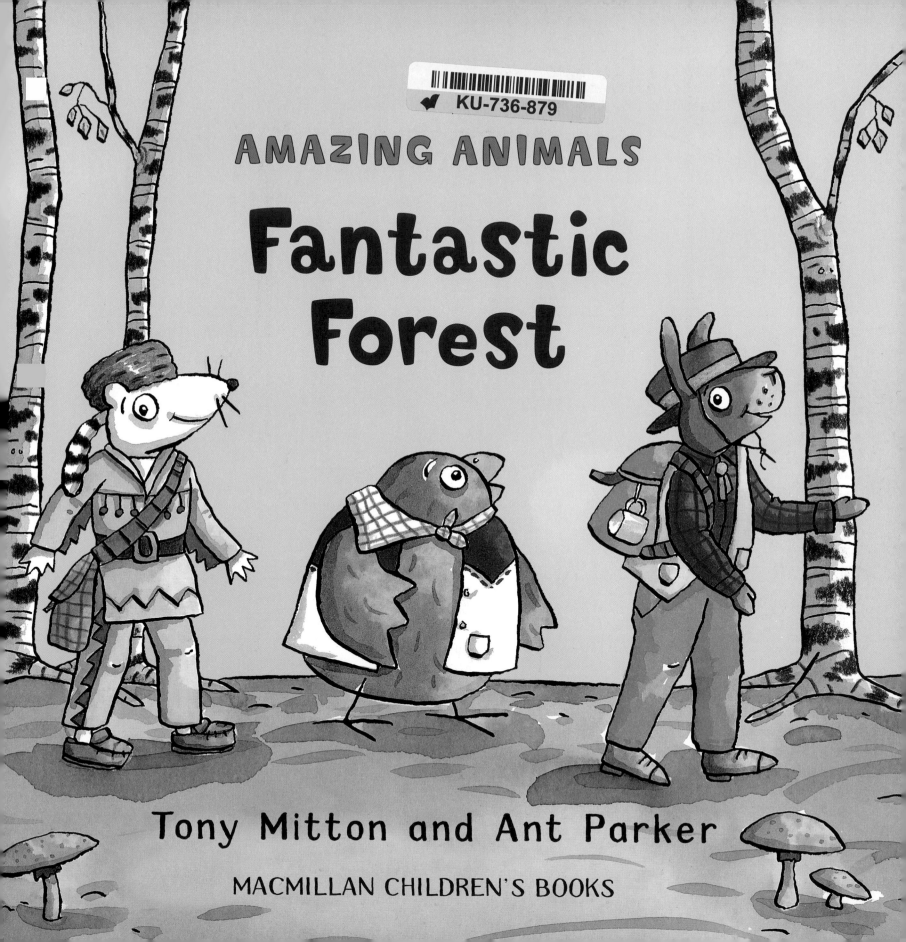

AMAZING ANIMALS

Fantastic Forest

Tony Mitton and Ant Parker

MACMILLAN CHILDREN'S BOOKS

In North American forests
many trees are evergreen.

And what a lot of creatures live there,
waiting to be seen!

Black bears are good at climbing.
Just see how well they do.

These bears are fetching insects
and pine cone nuts to chew.

Moose like eating water plants.
Their legs are long and thin.

When it's time for feeding,
they just go wading in.

When skunks are feeling threatened
they shoot a smelly spray.

The stink's so very strong
it drives most enemies away!

The graceful flying squirrel
can float from tree to tree.

Between its front and back legs
are flaps for gliding, see?

But look, the puma's prowling.
Keep quiet and stay well clear.

Though strong and fierce,
the puma's shy and mainly preys on deer.

The porcupine has sharp, barbed quills
that pierce fur or skin.

Most animals can't pull them out,
once they're sticking in!

Chipmunks love to nibble
on a berry, nut or seed.

They have to sleep through winter
so in summertime they feed.

The long-eared owl has two big tufts of feather on its head.

At dusk it swoops out hunting
when it's ready to be fed.

Our trip has shown us creatures
in trees or on the ground.

But if we take another look
which others can be found?

Did you find . . .

the lynx?

the crossbill?

the snowshoe hare?

the osprey?

the marten?

the beaver?

the wolverine?

the spruce
grouse?